TESSA SNYDER

Your Fourth Guide

First edition

This book was professionally typeset on Reedsy.
Find out more at reedsy.com

Contents

Preface	iv
Your Body	1
Feeding	18
Intimacy	22
Mommy Burnout	29
Support	34
MOM GUILT	45
Embodying YOUR Motherhood	49

Preface

Your "Fourth Trimester"

A guide to help navigate
your first 3 months postpartum.

Written with love, by Tessa Snyder

Congratulations! You just had a baby. It's an indescribable experience, in all honesty.

The emotions and hormones running through your body are really, really hard to sort through and even harder to talk about out loud because you can feel a little crazy with how conflicting the feelings can be.

How can you be exactly where you're meant to be, and further from yourself than you've ever been, at the same exact time? But that is just a "for instance", maybe that is not what you're experiencing at all.

Nobody knows what you're going through... except for you.

So take a deep breath, and know that no matter the experience, it's all completely normal and has been done by mother's before you everywhere. You are never alone in this.

These words are here to help you, well, guide yourself through this "Fourth" Trimester. We will discuss some things you may go through as the days go by and we'll have some prompts and exercises for you to do, so have a pen nearby if you can.

The way this guide is written is in no particular order. You do not have to follow along page by page as it is not a story with details to miss.

This guide is for you, so flip through the pages and prompts and do the ones that resonate with you in the moment. Do them every day if you need to, and revisit them if you feel like it.

This is about you, because when a child is born, so is a mother.

Your Body

As the "fourth" trimester progresses, your body will continue to change and so will how you feel towards it. It's encouraged to visit this chapter often to check in with yourself.

Go ahead and answer the question, without too much thought, just the first thing that comes to your mind, right now, right where you're at.

How do you feel about your body right now?

____

* * *

Take a moment to reflect on what you wrote you down. Be mindful of it now. Remember, you were prompted to answer without much thought, so now that you've answered, don't just rush past it. Roll it around.

Do you like this feeling? Do you wish to change it? Do you want to hold onto it forever?

Whatever your answers are, they are yours. They are not wrong. They are not the only ones. They can absolutely change.

Something I'd like to focus on in this chapter is taking your mind off of your *body image* and putting your focus onto your *life experience.*

Too often we forget what our bodies do and focus on how they look.

It's mentally draining on a new mom to be flooded with images of people and products that focus on "getting your body back".

You never lost your body. You are not less than you were before you got pregnant. You must not forget that it is just a marketing strategy to make you *feel* this way. To get you to spend money.

Say out loud: *Society preys on postpartum women to sell products and make money. It is nothing that is wrong with me, and everything that is wrong with society.*

Body image is just a marketing scheme.

List 3 things your body is doing right now that you're grateful for:

- ____

- ____

- ____

Just writing down "my eyeballs are reading this page right now" is something your body is doing for you that you don't often think about because it's so automatic. Just like breathing.

The little things are often the biggest things, don't discount them.

Remember to be mindful here. Reflect on your answers. How often do you think about them? Did you just recognize them? Are any of them new things that have come with motherhood? Which one makes you smile the most?

What is one thing your body can do for you today that will make you feel happy?

What is one thing you can do for your body today that will make it feel good?

Put into practice -

At the end of every day, whisper to yourself, "Thank you."

Thank your body for getting you through the day. For waking up, for getting up, for doing any function at all. Your body does not need to be measured in any kind of metric unit to be worthy of love and gratitude. It is worthy of all the love and gratitude right now. Just the way it is. Just the way you are.

You are worthy of all the love and gratitude.

* * *

Sprinkled throughout this guide are small coloring pages. Coloring has been proven to help adults take focus off of stressors and almost incite a meditative state, as you focus on the here and now of what you're doing. This is important for a new mother, who often struggles with thinking ahead and accomplishing long task lists. Relish in the here and now and remain mindful of the present moment. As they say, tomorrow isn't promised. Be here now.

What is my favorite memory before I got pregnant?

____

What was my favorite memory while I was pregnant?

____

What is my favorite postpartum moment so far?

____

Again, take time to reflect on your answers now. Do the memories make you smile? Make you laugh? Make you proud? When you think of these memories, what are the details you remember most? Maybe the way the room or air smelled? Maybe the way someone laughed or said something? Were they just of you? Were there other people there?

At any point in these memories, did you think about your body? Did you think about how strong it was? How capable? Did you think of the power? The grace? The beauty? The femininity? The softness?

Or did you find yourself not thinking of your body at all? Only on the joy the memories brought you?

This reflection time is to help you understand what you focus energy on and if you're okay with that energy being put there. So ask yourself, *"do I really want to spend any of my precious energy being worried about how my body looks?"*

This guide has been written based on the experiences of mothers before you and almost all of them struggled with their body image afterbirth. Scrolling through social media or skimming magazine covers at the grocery store leave no question as to why.

HOWEVER, the way your body ***looks*** to you is all based on how you ***feel*** towards it. Give yourself and your body a round of fucking applause because you, more than anybody in this entire universe, deserve YOUR LOVE and RESPECT.

The way you subconsciously speak to yourself will directly affect the relationship you have with your body. When you ***believe*** you're a badass, you see your body as sexy. When you embrace that you're powerful, you see your body as strong and capable.

When you speak to yourself, your body hears you, and at some point, she begins to believe you.

* * *

Be mindful of the way you talk to yourself. Do you empower yourself?

You will right now.

Use this space to write out some badass words of empowerment.

HYPE YOURSELF UP, GODDESS!

* * *

Let's check in!

Date: ____________________

Today I feel……

Today I am…….

Today I want……..

Today I will…….

Tomorrow…… will wait. **Just focus on today.**

* * *

It's a very tough journey to overcome the societal "rules" and "standards" placed on a woman. Not only that, the learned behaviors we grew up on. The things we heard and saw while we were just children ourselves ingrained themselves deep into our memory banks to shape the way we see and think of ourselves right now.

The way our mothers spoke and saw themselves, the TV shows we watched, the idols we looked up to, the friends we grew up with, and even THEIR mothers, all soaked into our veins and mental behavior.

Mindfulness will come up a lot in this book because it can really help you to recognize triggers and habits that have driven you on autopilot for so long. When you're in postpartum, the veil is lifted, and it can feel like you're being drowned in hot water...or trampled by bulls...or run over by a train... you get the idea.

When you have moments of guilt or disdain towards your body, try to stop for a second and ask yourself why.

For example:

Why do I feel guilty for eating this when I really wanted to have it?

Why do I hate the way I look right now when my body grew and then delivered human life?

Why do I feel upset that my old clothes still don't fit me just right?

When you stop and ask yourself these kinds of questions, you may surprise yourself with the answers. Sometimes, those answers won't actually have anything to do with you. Instead, they may all have something to do with *expectations you have created in your mind.*

Expectations that you need to have a "transformation body" *uh...newsflash.. your body has already done that...*

Expectations that you "have to do it all." *Cleaning, cooking, taking care of baby, yourself, your partners needs, work a job to contribute to the financial stability of the household, and YES, find time to workout so you can get....skinny... ?!*

Like...WHAT?

who the fucking hell set these expectations?

....Probably a man...

Which meaaaaannnnssss, you do not have to "abide" by these expectations. They're not realistic. Especially if you also work outside of the home. You are not a robot. AND, you're not hear to live this life based on the vanity of your body... are you?

I rope mindfulness in with expectations because we don't often realize where these expectations are coming from. During postpartum, it feels like they're coming from all different directions and you just can't seem to come up for any air. When we begin to be mindful, and we take a minute to just sit and breathe deeply, we can start to uncover where they're coming from.

You aren't going to be able to do the things you "used to do". No matter how determined you are to do it, even if you feel like you can conquer the entire world while baby naps. If you are used to being the one that does in fact, "Do it all", you will need to be especially mindful during the coming months.

I would like you to put into practice the process of S.T.O.P.

Stop-
Stop what you're doing and thinking.

Take a deep breath-
Clear your mind and bring yourself some calming energy.

Observe-
Observe your feelings. Observe your surroundings. Observe

your thoughts.

Proceed mindfully-

Ask yourself what and why.

"What is it that's causing me to feel this way and why am I choosing to react to it in this way?"

Try to practice this anytime you have some negative feelings bubble up. Whenever you feel guilty, angry, resentful, sad, or overwhelmed - stop.

In complete honesty, it's a tough habit to put into practice, but one of the most powerful tools you can have at your disposal in any situation. Proceeding mindfully can help you trace behaviors back to their source. Sometimes, our thoughts and actions are defense mechanisms that we've put in place to help us survive - to keep us safe.

It's human nature to stay comfortable. We are designed to return to a state of comfort and safety. When our bodies get too hot, we sweat to cool off. When they get dehydrated, we crave water to satiate. When they get tired, they force us to sleep.

So often our reactions to others, and even ourselves, are just mechanisms our body has adapted to using in an effort to maintain "homeostasis" within us.

When we have a baby? Our hormones are desperately working to "fix" the discomfort and it can feel like a roller coaster. Your body is working really, really hard now. So stop.

Stop expecting yourself to do it all, be it all, and have it all together.

What is just one thing I want to practice being more

mindful of?

Let's practice. Look at your answer. Hold it in your mind. Take a deep breath. Observe how it makes you feel. Proceed with the questions, what and why. See where it takes you.

What have I discovered about myself that mindfulness helped me to unveil?

How can I be more mindful of the thoughts I have towards my body?

---

* * *

While it's totally okay to have expectations and standards for yourself, the only expectations and standards you **should** place on yourself while postpartum, are *rest and recovery.*

Now, don't read what was not said.

Again, your expectations should be rest and recovery. If you do more than that, awesome! Sleeping, showering, taking it easy, staying in bed all day... that is all rest and recovery and nothing to feel guilty over, especially when these are the only expectations you've given yourself.

You will always be accomplished at the end of the day if your only expectation is resting and recovering.

What expectations have I placed on myself?

____

What is just one expectation I can let go of today so that I can better focus on rest and recovery?

____

Give yourself your grace. Give yourself your time. Give yourself your love. Give yourself your respect.

Give yourself forgiveness.

Forgiveness isn't just saying sorry. Forgiveness is choosing to let go of the expectation you upheld and no longer letting the burden of not meeting it weigh you down. So let go. Surrender. Forgive yourself for anything that may be weighing on you.

I forgive myself for ...

____

____

____

In the empty space of the mandala, write one word that you want to embody. Just one. As you color, see that word and think of its meaning. Absorb it. Breathe with it.

You can do hard things, mama.

* * *

Check in!

Date ______________________________

Today I feel…..

Today I want……

Today I will……

Today I'm grateful for……

Tomorrow… will wait. Just focus on today.

YOUR BODY

* * *

Feeding

However you feed your baby, know that you are doing an amazing job. You are the mother that your baby needs and you're doing the best you can; and that will always be good enough.

It's very tough to breastfeed, even if you have a lot of access to resources like lactation consultants, doctors, doulas, midwives, or classes. It's physically painful to have a baby attached to your nipples for more than half a day and a breast pump for a quarter of the time you have left. You're sore, cracked, and probably leaking.

You are more than a boob, even if you feel otherwise.

Mentally, breastfeeding or exclusively pumping can make you feel like you aren't in control of yourself or that your body isn't yours. Your life is being dictated by whenever your baby wants to nurse. Everything you do has to be planned around the feeding schedule and even when you get a long "break", maybe someone offers to let you nap or sleep in, you must pump or express because you're full and engorged or you still need to maintain a schedule to keep up your supply.

Or, in contrast, you don't feel engorged at all, and you're so stressed out that you aren't producing enough milk, how can you possibly sleep when you could be using that time to pump or produce?!

HOW FRUSTRATING!

Breastfeeding might not work for you. **That is okay.**

Your baby may continuously struggle to latch on, which causes you pain and stress as you just can't figure out why.

Emotionally, you're just so tired. There are so many hormones running through your body and so little sleep to help process them. It seems almost impossible to get any time for yourself to "catch up." You hear constantly, *"It is so worth it! Focus on these moments! Keep pushing! Keep going!"* And while everyone is only trying to be encouraging and supportive, it's invalidating you. Your feelings matter. Your struggles matter. Your life matters. YOU MATTER.

OF COURSE – this will not last. It DOES pass. You know that, I know that, everyone knows that. It doesn't make you ungrateful to recognize and acknowledge how difficult it is.

The days and the nights are so long right now.

You just have to figure out what works best for you and your baby and everyone else's opinions can bounce off of you – because **they** don't matter. If you want to hold and snuggle your baby all hours of the day, do it. If you want to let them self-soothe, do it. If you want to bottle feed, formula feed, pump, breastfeed, or some combination of all of those, do it. Use your motherly instinct and do what you need to do to take care of yourself and baby the best way you can.

You're doing a great job.

If you're measuring success in ounces, which is so common for new mothers, it may be time to evaluate your options.

If you're not finding any joy in breastfeeding or pumping whatsoever, it is okay to feed formula. You are not a failure for not being able to breastfeed or pump. You're not a failure in any sense. You're a mother, just trying to do what's best for your baby...

but please don't forget to do what's best for you.

It is not selfish of you to not breastfeed. It doesn't always happen and that is why other options exist. If you're really struggling, it is 100% okay to try another route.

Your mental health is more important than breastmilk.

How am I feeling about my boobs right now?

____

How can I make this experience more enjoyable for me?

____

Draw some simple doodles of your boobs below.

What is my favorite part about feeding time?

____

What do I want to remember about feeding time?

____

FEEDING

* * *

Intimacy

Your Vagina or C-Section

FIRST OFF, delivering a baby is HARD. There is no right or wrong way to do it. Your body has changed completely, your insides have moved and shifted around, and your uterus has taken a beating. It's going to hurt like hell and it's going to take TIME to recover. Do not let anyone dictate how much time it should or shouldn't take you. What took one mom 6 weeks could take another 2 years.

As discussed, this process is YOURS. You WILL grow through it. Don't compare, don't compete, and don't push or rush yourself. You must remember that there's no "getting back to" and instead, start thinking "growing into."

You are growing into a new version of you; mind, body, and soul. Don't look back at who you used to be and think of that as a destination, because that's your past, and you can't get back to it. Look ahead, instead, to a new, wiser, smarter, more profound, more powerful, stronger, and fierce woman. Because you're blossoming all the time.

Speaking of blossoms, your vagina or your tummy are probably a hot mess right now, and feel like anything but a beautiful flower.

Everything hurts, it's like you've been hit by a train, pooping is an Olympic sport, and it's hard to even think about sex.

OH MY GOSH. SEX.

Yes. The thing that created your little bundle of joy in the first place.

The advice here? Just take care of yourself. Just because your doctor clears you for sex and exercise doesn't mean you *have* to be ready to engage in the activities.

Speak to your partner about sex. It's going to feel different. It's going to look different. It's going to just be different, like most things in your life at this point. That is normal. That is okay. You are not weird or unloving or unlovable. Like discussed, you're just growing!

Or maybe you're super excited to start having sex again. You miss sex. Somewhere in this pressure-filled world sexuality in women has become a kind of taboo subject. You don't find a lot of people speaking about a woman's sexual appetite, her craving for pleasure and ecstasy . Why this has become such a taboo topic is a mystery to me. We women have so much to offer, so much to give. Our vagina's have been downplayed greatly. I know this sounds a little weird, but being postpartum and healing from birth shouldn't diminish the great power that can come from our vagina. Have you ever reveled in what you can do to a partner when it comes to your vagina? You can quite literally bring them to their knees.

Yes, postpartum is messy and complicated and...different. It's hard for women to be in a sexual place when emotions play such a big part in our sexual prowess. Your hormones and thoughts are all over the place right now and it's normal to feel out of sorts, but don't forget your power. Let's get some thoughts out on paper and sort through them.

The thought of sex right now makes me feel....

When I'm ready for sex again, I would love to...

When I'm ready for sex again, I would love for my partner....

My favorite part about sex is/was....

A fantasy I have right now is....

---

* * *

Intimacy doesn't just have to be about sex or sexual acts. Holding hands, looking into each other's eyes, or getting a foot rub are all forms of intimacy.

However, something to be discussed is being "touched out". When you've been holding onto your baby all day because they refused to be put down for even a second, then when you finally get a second of peace to yourself, your partner wants to cuddle or hug or have an intimate moment and you're screaming, *"No thank you!"*

You find yourself completely irritated that your partner wants you to do these things right now.

Feeling touched out just means you've been touched all day and that you just want time to **yourself**. To just breathe your own air. To take up your own space. It is completely normal among all mothers to feel this way. Your partner may not understand this and they could be hurt by your rejections, which just causes unnecessary strain on your relationship. Being familiar with this term is important in communicating *why* you don't feel like hugging and kissing or being intimate with them at that time.

You can explain to them that after being constantly needed by your baby all day long, it's just nice to have a moment to do something alone. After speaking about it, you can find a compromise somewhere. Maybe they can draw you a bath, you can share a meal together, or they can just let you have this time to yourself and let you come to them when you're ready. But if you don't speak about it, your partner feels isolated and eventually, so do you. You're not a mind reader and neither is anyone else. Communicating these very real, and very valid, feelings, is the only way to keep everyone on the same page.

"Mommy burnout" is another real phenomenon that happens with postpartum. You could feel like you're juggling everything all the time, and nobody is making time or effort to help you or understand you. This can lead to resentment and anger, which, in turn, leads to more exhaustion and less intimacy.

In the later years, mommy burnout can look like constant anger; yelling and being frustrated when your kids aren't listening. Having thin patience and a short fuse.

It's been proven now that "self-care" is simply not enough to "cure" mommy burnout, as much of it is caused from external, societal and cultural, factors, so being mindful of your feelings and communicating them out loud is very important. You're going to have to be vulnerable and honest with what you think, feel, and need, especially when it comes to your partner.

Again, society has painted this picture that women must do it all. That mother's chose this life, so they better be able to handle it with a smile on their face and gratitude in their voice.

That's just not realistic. Or fair. It's not fair to your partner, to your family, and most of all, it's not fair to you. Don't believe in this bullshit that you're not allowed to ask for help. That you're not allowed to cry in front of people. That's you're not allowed to breakdown every once in awhile. YOU ARE. YOU CAN. YOU SHOULD.

I talk about "Touched Out" and "Mommy Burnout" in relation to intimacy because it plays a huge role in your intimate relationships. We are only human. We only have so much room in hearts, minds, and souls to give and receive before we ultimately hit Empty.

Recognizing these feelings and setting boundaries with others in our lives can help us direct focus to our partner, as well as to us. Let's face it, when the moment is right and you feel safe and loved, sex is awesome. It's just as healthy and beneficial to us as it is to our partners. So don't feel like you can't talk about what's affecting you in the bedroom department.

Your sexual health is important, too! What do you *need* to feel pleased? Do you need words of affirmation? Do you need your ass grabbed more? Do you need your boobs left alone? Do you just need a hot shower alone?

Do you feel like you're experiencing "Touched Out"?

What is something you can do for just yourself, right now?

Do you feel connected with yourself?

Do you feel like being Touched Out or Burned out is affecting your intimacy?

What are other forms of intimacy(not sex) I can speak to my partner about enjoying with me?

Let's come back to mindfulness here. Take a few deep breaths. Sit in this moment. Reflect on your answers. How are you feeling? Are the prompts helping you sort out your thoughts or give you any ideas or clarity? Do you feel a million miles away? Are you trying to split your time and energy on multiple projects or are you right here, right now?

Every moment is fleeting. Take time throughout your day to just be where you are, doing what you're doing. Don't be thinking about what's next, what's tomorrow, or what's next week. There will always be time to do that.

Try to keep your mind where your body is.

Mommy Burnout

Mommy burnout gets its own chapter because it's so important to be able to recognize and acknowledge in yourself. I find that it mostly comes from societal expectations. Yes, those pesky expectations, again. When you begin to believe them, you put those same expectations on yourself, then, when you can't do it, you feel like a total failure. Don't carry these feelings alone. Don't let your ego get in the way of asking for help. And don't let other people make you feel like you're "just complaining" and "you just need to focus on the positives." THIS is a big factor that leads to mommy burnout and it can really affect your relationships.

These months are where it's really important to learn how to set emotional boundaries.

As defined -

Emotional boundaries involve separating your feelings from another's feelings. Violations include -

- taking responsibility for another's feelings

- letting another's feelings dictate your own
- sacrificing your own needs to please another
- blaming others for your problems and accepting responsibility for theirs

Becoming a mother makes you responsible for another human being. This heightens your ability for empathy so you end up projecting that responsibility onto everyone else. You want to take care of people, to make them happy, to create peace. Remember that this isn't your job. Your job is to take care of you and baby. That's it. Yes, it's important to nurture your relationships and ask for support, but without healthy boundaries, these relationships can do you more harm than good.

Your mom or mother-in-law comes by to help out and just keeps giving you relentless advice on how you **should** be doing things.

A boundary can look something like, "I appreciate your advice and I'd also appreciate it if you could just respect my decisions as a mother."

Or it could be as simple as just saying, "No."

You don't owe anyone any explanations. Ever. The people that deserve to be in your life will understand and respect that. The ones that get offended or demand reasoning? Well, that's entirely up to you where those people belong. You've got enough going on in your life right now without the added stress of "people pleasing" everyone but yourself.

Mommy burnout can make you resentful to motherhood. It

feels like there's no end in sight to the duties you need to accomplish and the things you need to get done. You get on social media and see everyone's picture perfect children and their picture perfect lives and you wonder why you can't do that or have that. Why isn't your house that clean? Why is your baby constantly spitting up on your clothes so you can't even wear something nice?

Give yourself **social media boundaries**, too! Take a break. Get off of it completely or at least mute/unfollow every page that makes you feel bad or inferior. Follow new pages. New people. Real, raw, unedited mothers showing their truths in motherhood if you can find them. Women you can **relate** to not *compare* to. If you find yourself comparing, return to S.T.O.P.

Stop
-Stop what you're doing and thinking.

Take a deep breath
-Clear your mind and bring yourself some calming energy.

Observe
-Observe your feelings. Observe your surroundings. Observe your thoughts.

Proceed mindfully
-Ask yourself what and why.

"What is it that's causing me to feel this way and why am I choosing to react to it in this way?"

Do you feel like you're experiencing mommy burnout?

Where do you feel the expectation to "do it all" is coming from?

What is one thing you can do this week, alone, to help alleviate any pressure you feel?

What do you honestly feel like saying when someone asks "How are you?"

Do you need more support in order to feel more intimate?

Use this space to write out everything you ever wanted to say to people who gave you unsolicited advice and you chose to bite your tongue instead...

* * *

Check in!

Date:______________

I'm feeling.....

I want to.....

I need.....

I'm grateful for....

Tomorrow will....
wait. Focus on today.

Support

Postpartum women are some of the most unsupported people in America. The expectations(there's that word again) that you should be able to jump right back up into life like you didn't just have a baby is complete bullshit. Throw it out. Light it on fire. That is NOT what you should be doing. Don't expect that of yourself and don't let others expect that of you either. You need to take all the time YOU need to fully recover and settle into your new life as a mother, and you need to be able to SPEAK UP about that need!

Now, I get it. A lot of us need to return to work after our 6 week disability partial pay to help pay the bills. Not to mention the added stress of childcare, which is something that you and your partner need to sit down and talk about, sooner rather than later.

There's a cultural blackhole out there that says we must hustle, hustle, hustle to prove we are worth something(Mommy burnout!)

Guess what? You don't have to do shit to prove shit to anyone.

Stand in your worthiness right now. Because you are worthy as you are, in this moment.

Asking for support in a world that doesn't offer it freely is TOUGH. It is uncomfortable to admit struggles, to admit that you're having a hard time, that you need help. People can seem surprised, disappointed, or worse, they make it about them somehow... like, how do people manage to do that?

Anyways.

This chapter is all about figuring out the kind of support you need. Sometimes the support you need is small, like words of affirmation from someone else telling you you're doing a great job.

Sometimes, it's your favorite coffee or tea from your local coffee shop.

Sometimes, it's both of those things while you're taking a hot bath with a face mask while someone massages your feet, feeds you grapes, gives you money to go shopping, holds you while you sob uncontrollably, and then watches the baby while you nap for 4 hours before going to see a therapist.

Sometimes it's something much larger, like not returning to work so soon. Or childcare. Those two things are perfect examples of how unnurturing society has become, and those things are not your fault. They are not for you to carry alone. All mother's stand with you in solidarity on that front.

This chapter will mainly focus on support from your partner. Facilitating communication so that you can better understand each other in this new phase of parenthood.

****Exercises in this chapter are constructed to be worked through with a partner. If you're a single mom, you can ask a friend or a family member that you'd love support from, or if you don't want to do that, or can't, it is totally okay to work through them on your own or skip entirely.

It can be tough to communicate what you need when you don't *really* know what it is. Or worse, you know exactly what it is you need but you don't know how to communicate it or feel like you shouldn't be asking for it.

Whatever the dilemma, you should be reminded, once again, **this is all totally normal to experience.**

Sometimes it can feel like your whole entire life has had this huge shift and everything has changed for you, but your partner's life appears to haven't changed at all. You start finding resentment in the nighttime awakenings, watching your partner sleep soundly while you're awake, once again, feeding/changing/burping/rocking the baby.

Your partner may go off to work and do their normal hobbies, returning home to laundry left undone and food uncooked. You both feel frustrated as you only see the outside of what's happening, somehow ending up in a competition of who has it harder.

Honestly, this chapter could go on and on with examples such as this, but you catch the drift. There's a lot of emotions going on and if left untouched, those emotions only fester.

Obviously, not everyone experiences the same things. Maybe these particular examples don't resonate with you and that's okay!

Use the prompts to put MORE focus on those positives and continue to generate gratitude!

How supported do I feel right now?

What would make me feel more supported?

What is one thing that I can do to better support myself?

What is one thing my partner can do to better support me?

I really want to talk to my partner about...

Remember to look back at your answers and reflect on how they make you feel. Take deep breaths in and out while you read them and let them settle before moving on. Use the space below to jot down any other notes about things you'd like to talk about.

Now is the time to bring your partner in! There is no such thing as a perfect time or place, so just let your partner know you'd love their help in these exercises. If you can, sit with one another, no phones, no outside distractions, during a time when it's quiet for both of you.

We're going to start these prompts with an easy meditation, so you're both calm and in tune with yourselves. Remember, these are to come from spaces of love. If at any point, it turns into a competition of who is doing what, someone becomes defensive, or it becomes argumentative, stop. Come back to the mediation, start again.

These prompts are simply here to help **facilitate conversation** between the new mom and dad. What mom needs may not be what dad thinks she needs, and vice versa.

There are spaces to write your answers, but don't feel like you have to. Writing them down is a great way to remember what each of you has said and you can return to them later if you need the reminder.

Begin -

Start with a deep breath – in through the nose, filling the stomach with air, and slowly out through the mouth.

Close your eyes.

Imagine you are butter sitting on a windowsill. The sun pouring through the window is golden and warm and you begin to soften up.

Slowly melting into your space.

Stay here, in this warmth, in this softness, for a few deep breaths.

When you both feel relaxed, move onto the next page.

How are you feeling about parenthood right now?

:____

____

:____

____

How are you feeling about our connection right now?

:____

____

:____

____

What is something I do that you appreciate the most?

:____

____

:____

____

What is something that you are silently struggling with right now?

:____

____

:____

____

What is something I can do to better support you?

:____

____

:____

____

What are 3 things you're grateful for right now?

:____

____

:____

____

What is one thing you could hear me say more often?

:____

____

:____

____

How are you feeling about our levels of intimacy right now?

:____

____

:____

____

Do you feel like this exercise has helped us better understand each other's needs?

:____

____

:____

____

Let's take a break here. Reflect on the answers. Do you feel like the questions helped to facilitate open conversation? Do you feel more supported? At ease? A little more understood?

* * *

Let's do a mommy check-in….

Date: ____________________

I feel…….

I want…….

I will……

Tomorrow…..will wait. **Just focus on today.**

* * *

*If you fear your partner or are being abused (mentally or physically) please call the national domestic violence hotline at 1-800-799-7233 or chat with an advocate online at their website.

You are never alone. You are worthy of all the love in the world.

"Fear is only a feeling; it cannot hold me back."

* * *

Nobody except you knows what you are feeling or thinking right now. Nobody knows how to best support you except for you. So you have to speak up and ask for it.

When you were pregnant, everyone asked you what you needed and just wanted to be there to help you out and when you give birth, it seems like everyone just asks about the baby and what they can do to help you… with the baby.

You, too, are still here. You, too, still need support and help. You, too, still need attention.

And YES. You, too, DESERVE IT.

Keep speaking up until you get it. From your partner, from your friends, from your family, from your doctor, from yourself.

Don't ever give up searching and asking for support no matter how uncomfortable you may feel about it.

Let the veil come down and stand, proudly, in your vulnerability.

If you feel like you have depression and you are having really hard thoughts, please reach out to a doctor about your concerns. You don't have to take medication if you don't want to, but you need to ask for resources that can help you get through.

This guide journal is here to help you navigate through postpartum with words and mindful intentions. Sometimes you need more than that and that is OKAY. That is NORMAL. It will be reiterated again and again, **This. Shit. Is. HARD.**

If you're struggling, don't struggle alone. Don't fight alone. Not that you can't, because you can definitely punch, kick, and claw your way out of any darkness, but that you shouldn't have to.

* * *

Check in with yourself, mama!

Date: ____________________

I feel……

I want……

I love……

I laugh when……

I smile when…….

I am grateful for……..

MOM GUILT

Mom guilt is a doozy to navigate. It's a constant anxiety of "Did I really do my best? Could I have done more? Is this the right way? The best way?" It honestly never ends.

And it only gets worse as your baby grows.

Mom guilt is another thing I can assure you is normal among mom culture. And to be honest, I don't have much advice for it, as I, too, struggle with it.

The advice I do have is this -

At the end of every night, take a deep breath.

Now think about this -

How many snuggles did you get today?

How many smiles did you share?

Were there moments of just you and baby, alone but present with each other?

Remember how they smell.

Remember how they look at you.

Remember how much you love them.

Remember how much they love you.

It's easy to get sucked into mom guilt and anxiety. To feel like everything you're doing is never enough or that you could always be doing better. I think it usually ties back into those pesky expectations we place on ourselves. If we can focus on the positives of the day, of all the things that we're grateful for, that made us happy, then we can start to change our lives.

Life after baby doesn't HAVE to be so hard, does it?

It doesn't HAVE to feel like one hurdle after another that we can barely manage to jump over. We're fucking amazing. We're women. We deserve better.

What is one thing you're grateful for today?

What is one thing you feel guilty about?

Why do you feel guilty?

What's something else you're grateful for today?

Let's use this time to reflect back on your answers. Is the guilt you're feeling tied to an expectation? Is what you're grateful for more important than your guilt?

Remember, guilt is just a feeling. As is anxiety. You experience these things, they are not part of you. You don't have to take ownership of them.

"I'm anxious."

"I'm sad."

That's like saying, "I AM anxiety. I AM sadness." Those aren't you. That's not who you are. You are not a feeling.

Instead say, "I'm experiencing some feelings of guilt around this right now."

"I'm having some feelings of anger."

"I'm sensing feelings of anxiety here."

By posing your brain to think in this way, you can almost trick yourself into letting them pass.

Feelings are temporary if you let them be.

You're going to be experiencing a lot of different feelings. A lot of different thoughts. A lot of different paths to take. The best one is the one you decide on. The best ones are the ones that keep you and baby safe, fed, rested, and alive.

You're doing an amazing job.

* * *

Check in!

Date: ____________________

Right now I feel...

I am grateful for...

My feelings are...

I think....

Tomorrow I will.... wait. Focus only on today.

Embodying YOUR Motherhood

By this time, you've probably thought a lot about the kind of mother you want to be. How you want to raise your baby, teach your baby, and be the example for your baby.

At this stage, everyone has an opinion. We won't even get into examples of opinions you've probably already heard. Remember that the only opinion that matters is yours -

What do you want to do? What do you want to try?

The answer?

Whatever makes you happiest.

Motherhood is magical and chaotic and ugly and beautiful. It is full of stumbles, fumbles, growth, opportunities, and pure love. It is the best and the hardest job you will ever do.

It's important in this "fourth trimester" to keep learning about mindfulness and how to stay present in the moment you are in.

Take a moment here, to look at this page.

Feel the paper. Feel the book. Think about where you got this book from. How many do you think touched it? How long did it take to write? Was the mother writing this book going through her own struggles just like me? What tree, in what forest, was cut down to make this paper? How was the seed planted?

When you sit for a moment and think about the cycles of life, you can realize how much must happen for this one moment to occur. In this one moment, you were meant to be here. Doing exactly this. Everything that has happened externally in the universe has come together, to put you right here.

How completely mind blowing.

When your baby is up in the middle of the night again, crying, seemingly inconsolable, and you're exhausted and frustrated, think about all those things that had to come together to put you in that moment. To give you this baby. To make you this mother.

You were meant to be this mother.

* * *

Let's check in!

Date: _________________________

When I think about being a mother, I feel....

____

When I think about myself outside of being a mother, I am...

____

My favorite part about being a mom so far is...

My favorite part about myself as a mom is...

Motherhood so far has been....

I would love to start...

Use this space here to write out any thoughts, feelings, or vibes you have. Write yourself some words of encouragement, empowerment, and love.

* * *

Sometimes it can feel as if you're rushing to get back to some sense of your old self. Your old habits, routines, and identity.

Nobody seems to tell you that it is totally okay to let all of that go. While it's amazing to have goals, they shouldn't be focused on going backwards.

I'm here to tell you right now that it's okay to let go of who you used to be. That there's an even better version of you right here, right now.

You are not the same woman you were before you got pregnant nor should you try to get back to her, because you never will. Stop searching. Stop looking for her in every mirror, in every photo, in every face.

Stop expecting her to return with every workout, every old pair of jeans, every new strand of hair that grows back...

she's not coming back.

Instead, surrender into your motherhood and let the new woman you are becoming

find you.

You are absolutely beautiful. Completely loved. Abundantly supported.